Voices Of The Future

Edited By Wendy Laws

First published in Great Britain in 2020 by:

Young Writers
Remus House
Coltsfoot Drive
Peterborough
PE2 9BF
Telephone: 01733 890066
Website: www.youngwriters.co.uk

All Rights Reserved
Book Design by Ashley Janson
© Copyright Contributors 2020
Softback ISBN 978-1-83928-953-8

Printed and bound in the UK by BookPrintingUK
Website: www.bookprintinguk.com
YB0444K

FOREWORD

Here at Young Writers our defining aim is to promote the joys of reading and writing to children and young adults and we are committed to nurturing the creative talents of the next generation. By allowing them to see their own work in print we believe their confidence and love of creative writing will grow.

Out Of This World is our latest fantastic competition, specifically designed to encourage the writing skills of primary school children through the medium of poetry. From the high quality of entries received, it is clear that it really captured the imagination of all involved.

We are proud to present the resulting collection of poems that we are sure will amuse and inspire.

An absorbing insight into the imagination and thoughts of the young, we hope you will agree that this fantastic anthology is one to delight the whole family again and again.

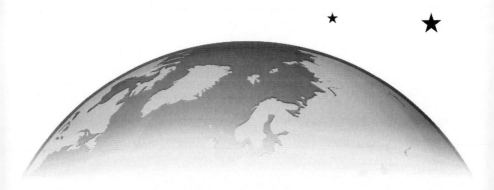

CONTENTS

St Andrew's CE Primary School, Plymouth

Makeda Williamson (8)	58
Hannah Ryder (8)	59
Rihanna Voronina (8)	60
Zylah Ford (8)	61
Loveday Hoskin (7)	62

St Mary's CE Junior School, Twickenham

Eric Paqvalen (10)	63
Amaya Maqsood (9)	64
Luciana Nico Siddique Bottomly (10)	66
Euan Offord (9)	68
Anna Wilkinson (9)	70
Gloria Makufi (10)	72
Alexander F E Harrison (9)	74
Sienna Mary Dane (9)	76
Rosie Mcmullen (10)	77
Charlotte Irvine (9)	78
Marco Gonzalez (9)	79
Lucy Goddin (10)	80
Ibuki Miyaji (9)	82
Gabriel Le Boiteux (9)	83
Alba Morrison (10)	84
Bibi Foxwood (9)	85
Max Tanawin Attwood (9)	86
Daniel Hammer (10)	87
Mollie-Rae Mo (9)	88
Lal Kuruyazici (10)	89
Owen Minty (9)	90
Izzy Mortimore (10)	91
Elise Cobb (10)	92
Frankie Montero (9)	93
Federico Prenovost (10)	94
Martha Swift (9)	95
Peter Deasy (10)	96
Ben John (10)	97
Josh Menassa Tye (10)	98
Matvey Yasser (10)	99
Camila Key Bianchin (9)	100

Poppy Frances Victoria Drew (9)	101
Heitor Rucco Turina (10)	102
Tai-Rhys Anthony Brown (10)	103

St Thomas CE Primary School, Boston

Grace Dada (9)	104
Isabelle Gutteridge (9)	105
Lyla Needham (9)	106
Ella Farmer (10)	107
Jessica Roofe (9)	108
Lily Cowell (9)	109
Libby-Jo Hurford (10)	110
Lola Ward (9)	111
Summer Parrott (9)	112
Stephen Williams (9)	113

Wharton Primary School, Little Hulton

Natalia Ogorzalek (9)	114
Jamie-Luke Georgiou (10)	116
Ethan Anderton (9)	117
Jesmira Kanjinga (10)	118
Amy Hricova (10)	119
Harli Oxton (9)	120
Logan Pendlebury (10)	121
Thomas Kennedy (10)	122
Jack Hamilton (10)	123
Harlie Penny (10)	124
Sheba Adebambo (10)	125
Shema Ngarambe (10)	126
Sophia Cahill (9)	127
Seanna Heidi Puddoo (9)	128
Julia Vernan (9)	129
Elle-May Riley (9)	130
Callum D'arcy (9)	131
Lucian Winder (9)	132
William Szelepa (10)	133

THE POEMS

What I Wish For, Hmm, I Don't Know

What I wish for, I don't know,
What I wish for are love and peace,
What I wish for, I don't know,
What I wish for is no more war.
What I wish for, I don't know,
What I wish for is that people sitting in wheelchairs
can stand once again and dance to the music they
can hear from miles away.
What I wish for, I don't know,
What I wish for is a new world where anyone can
enter with no pain,
With no sad tears in their eyes, but happy tears.
What I wish for, I don't know,
Wait!
I don't have any wishes because all my wishes
have come true,
In my head and in my heart and in the people I
love most,
There are no more wishes and no wishes should be
dark.

Abigail Agbontaen (9)
Brampton Primary School, East Ham

School Experiences

School is where you learn,
Lovely teachers come to help,
Sometimes maths is where we struggle,
If you don't progress then you're in trouble,
Teachers are there to solve your problems
And if you listen you avoid the trouble.

Break is when you rest
To have fruit is best,
You play for fifteen minutes
Which gets rid of all the fidgets,
You then come back to class,
Focused on your English task.

English is an important subject,
If you leave out punctuation,
The sentence goes on and on and on and on
And on and on
But when you use a comma,
You can slow down for a second here,
Using a full stop means we better just stop right
here.

Suddenly the bell rings,
It's time to go to class,
To finish off my English task,
So the science lesson can start.

Filling up cups with ice,
Watching them melt in size,
Keeping time of the change from a solid to a liquid,
Makes me feel like a true scientific whizz-kid.

It's the end of the day now that the lesson is done,
At last we go outside,
To go home and have some fun.

Polina Hector (9)
Brampton Primary School, East Ham

The Alluring Hideaway

Whose garden is that?
I think I know,
The owner is relaxing deeply though,
Their exquisite sanctuary reminds me of a vivid
rainbow.

The birds are tweeting
In wonderful greeting.
They sing so softly and gently,
As the trees listen silently.

When the blue summer sky begins to fade,
The warm flaming colours are being made.
And through the clouds, the sun is beaming,
The light shines as the old sundial is gleaming.

I see the dew set upon the grass
While I am peering through the glass,
A rabbit hopping gives a satisfying crunch,
While nibbling on its veggie lunch.

The flowers are attractive and bright,
The vibrant colours are nice and light,

Daffodils, violets, tulips and roses,
It is a delightful scent to our noses.

I gratefully indulge in this tranquil haven...

Inaya Hussain (10)
Brampton Primary School, East Ham

Football

Throwing the long ball, making the run,
Grabbing a tackle, having some fun.
Breaking a record, maybe some teeth,
Be in the pile on not underneath.
Pull in the long one, wave to the crowd,
Cuff your opponent, scream it out loud.
Run down the field till you turn blue,
Everything you hear might not be true.
Now and then you might break a rib,
Nowadays who needs a bib?
Turn for the handoff, dropping the ball,
What kind of person would make such a call?
Pulling some muscles, slammed to the ground,
Hoping that some day your eye will be found.
Slipping and sliding on grass full of goo
At least it's not as worse as poo!
So that's the fun of football.

Aayan Haseeb (10)
Brampton Primary School, East Ham

The Unicorn

When it's in the air
I groan with despair.
The twirl and whirl of its magical tail,
Stops all wars from happening.
Its lavish mane flipping everywhere,
Tells us what its mane and fur looks like.
Tufts of fluffy fur falling like snow,
Raises Britain's hopes up without letting them know.
Beams of rainbows zooming through the sky,
Spreads love and joy around the world.
The adorable unicorn has an amazing reputation,
With contagious cheer and all above.
Real or not real,
The unicorn is still alive in our minds as a fantasy.
The fluffy unicorn puts you to bed,
With magnificent, multicoloured visions running through your head.

Fitza Virk (10)
Brampton Primary School, East Ham

Super Multiple

This is Super Multiple,
He flies through the air like a sheet of paper
flapping,
His hands create anything he imagines,
Oh no, there's a fire in the building with a person
inside,
Here comes the action part,
Super Multiple is a thunderbolt in the sky,
He flies in and he rescues the person,
Now his hands create a hose,
He stops the fire,
Then he leaves the citizen on the ground,
Then he flies to his HQ,
Super Multiple's HQ is full of gadgets,
There's a shrinker, a laser gun,
Last but definitely not least, his giant screen.

Nicholas Blaga (9)
Brampton Primary School, East Ham

Lonely Boy

I am a lonely boy,
Life says to me,
"Come here, my boy."
"Yes."
I want to fly like a butterfly
To spread all colours to life and help others.

I am a lonely boy,
Death says to me,
"Come here, my boy."
"Yes."
Yes to break all the weakness and shyness
And to stop all the bullying and not to hurt.

I am a lonely boy,
God gives me good stuff,
Do not do anything bad.
I am one healthy boy
And one wealthy boy.

Alwin Sharley (10)
Brampton Primary School, East Ham

Feelings

Sometimes I'm happy,
Other times I'm sad.
Most of the time I'm glad,
But on a school day I'm bad.
During my maths lesson I get a bit confused,
But during my PE lesson I get a bit bruised.
When I get annoyed I find it best to avoid,
Never keep a problem inside,
It is never best to avoid.
Mental health may be just two words,
But to some people it could be the end of the world.
So listen and help when you can
Because you never know when they're down.

Rayleigh Taylor (10)
Brampton Primary School, East Ham

Shadows

Shadows,
Many shadows,
They say she's a shadow,
Fading, fading, fading,
Waiting, waiting, waiting,
Sitting there staring,
Not even glaring,
Black as night,
Light as day,
She's modelling clay,
Slowly fading away,
They say she's from the hollow,
Shadows,
Shadows,
Shadows,
Gloomy dark shadows.

Aleena Ullah (10)
Brampton Primary School, East Ham

Back In The Days

Back in the day when it was cool
Poor people worked on stools.
What was it like back in the day
In the trendy 1930s and the dirty 1940s?
Was life lame
When they didn't have video games?
Could only rich people hitch car rides?
Was Queen Victoria a queen lawyer?
Did ancient Greeks reek?
What were life and strife back in the day?

Noli Pagaduan (9)

Brampton Primary School, East Ham

The Dark Angel

We feel happy but sometimes sad,
Sometimes we're mad when we do something bad.
Sometimes we're lonely in the midnight sky,
That's the dark angel who makes us cry.
She is there, without her inner brightness
She causes moodiness.
She ruins adventures, with her little sparkly eyes
She sees someone crying.

Nana Asenso (9)
Brampton Primary School, East Ham

My Mum!

My mum is as sweet as rose gold cotton candy,
She helped me during the rain and wind,
She showers me with hugs and kisses,
During hard times she was unbelievably brave.
Her smile makes me feel like the luckiest girl.
She makes the sun shine every day with her smile.
She kisses my pain away, as I'm crying in sorrow.

Ganishka Umakumaran (10)

Brampton Primary School, East Ham

Planets

Above the night sky
Are big, large planets
Filled with nitrogen
Or maybe hydrogen.

Some have lava
some have ice
Some we don't know of
Some produce life.

Several aren't planets
They are stars
Or a dwarf planet
Chilling with the stars!

Riyan Salivendra (9)
Brampton Primary School, East Ham

Midnight Sky!

Moonbeams as a sapphire light,
Dancing around in the forest
Of the dreamy, galaxy sky!
Rolls lazily to find a place too,
To sleep with all the shimmery
Diamond stars singing a lullaby,
Of the heart of the jewel!

Urwa Ali (10)
Brampton Primary School, East Ham

My Beautiful Wee Cat, Midnight

There is a cat who lives in a hat.
She runs out onto the mat for me to give her a pat.
She likes eating rats and playing with cats.
She is a very fat cat who likes sitting on the mat.
She has beautiful fur and likes to purr.
She likes to drink milk and her fur is as soft as silk.
She loves fish in her dish and plenty of treats to eat.
When I call my cat, she comes like a bat.
Oh, I just love my cat, the silly wee brat, my cat.

My cat is called Midnight
And she is so light.
She likes a tasty bite
And sometimes she fights with Oreo, my other fat cat.
She is pure black and likes lying on her back,
She has green eyes and is keen to play with me,
My beautiful cat, Midnight.

Victoria Martin (9)
Kingsmills Primary School, Whitecross

One Leg Less!

I see a big brown, fierce killer bear.
I hear the crunch of the sticks snapping from under its paws.
I can almost taste the fear running through my veins.
I smell the blood dripping down its fangs
As it eats the body of a live deer!
I feel its paws wrapping around my body and squeezing me...
I think I am dead but I find myself in daylight but...

I have no leg, it ate my leg right off.
I have my phone, I get it and call 999,
It answers, I ask for a paramedic.
Good they're here! They'd come!
They take me to the hospital.

Three weeks later! I am going home today,
Never going to the forest again!

Matthew Fegan (10)
Kingsmills Primary School, Whitecross

Megalodon

A kennings poem

It's a wild animal,
A people-killer,
A blood-maker,
An ocean-owner,
A boat-hater,
A human-sniffer,
A sea-swimmer,
A body-blender,
A whale terror,
A ferocious monster,
A meat-eater,
A fish-catcher,
A beach-emptier,
A large animal,
A human-scarer,
A bone-cruncher
And an extinct creature.

Reuben Cartmill (10)
Kingsmills Primary School, Whitecross

The Blue Alien And The Boy

One day a blue alien came his way,
"Blue Alien," he said, "why do you look so sad?"
"This planet is bad!" he replied.
"It needs saving but only humans can decide."
The boy asked, "May I help you, please?
I will make an announcement to stop people using
plastic that will end up in the seas!
I'll be back soon, before the moon!"
The boy went to the Prime Minister at the House of
Lords.
He went there carrying his warning notice boards.
He told the blue alien, "I made everyone aware
We all should treat the world with good care."
The alien was happy and then turned yellow,
He waved bye-bye and flew off into the deep blue
sky.

Lexi-Mae Seal (9)
Nethersole CE Academy, Polesworth

Lost In Space

I went to space, that great big place,
I thought it might be fun.
I shot past Mars,
Then lots of stars,
Like a bullet from a gun.
My trusty ship, I'd named her Pip
Was caught by a black hole.
All my fears turned to tears
As my ship lost all control.
In I went, unconfident, deep into the gloom,
I closed my eyes but to my surprise,
This wasn't yet my doom.
I re-emerged, all perturbed, in a strange new universe,
Soon my grief became relief,
This day could have been worse.

Erin Davis
Nethersole CE Academy, Polesworth

The Earth Is Missing!

As the days go by, the time flies;
The stars shine as bright as the sun.
Then this...
A bright light beckons the Earth
To approach this mystical vortex of light.
What is the Earth about to behold?
Where will this lead? A place of mystery that needs to unfold.
As the planets, except for one, sit peacefully, unharmed,
One drifts towards the vortex of light,
That shines incredibly bright.
As the Earth gets rolled into the incredible source of light,
The Earth is no longer to be found...

Leah Wiggins (10)
Nethersole CE Academy, Polesworth

Sunflowers And Daisies

Sunflowers are tall
And daisies are small!
But they are both my favourite flowers of course!

Bees take the pollen
And make it into honey
So we can enjoy it every day
Without spending money.

Sunflowers and daisies
Are similar in ways
And take a lot of days
To grow!

Sunflowers are tall
And daisies are small
But they are both my favourite flowers of course!

Ellie May Drury (9)
Nethersole CE Academy, Polesworth

Rocket Day

Today is rocket day when rockets sweep the skies,
No one knows where they go, but they know
they're up so high.
Some people say they fly to space,
But some say they go to Mars,
Some people say they go to the moon,
But others think it's bizarre,
So today is rocket day when rockets sweep the
skies,
I don't know how to get through the day,
But I know I'll have to try!

Ashleigh May Mahood (9)
Nethersole CE Academy, Polesworth

The Day I Met John

I went to Mars on a satellite
That was out of control,
I met an alien called John
Who tried to take control.
When it stopped he said, "Bleep, bloop,"
And we became friends
And that was the end.

Izzy Barber (9)
Nethersole CE Academy, Polesworth

Peas In A Pod!

F acetime, funfair, plaiting each other's hair

R ainbows, riding bikes, skating on a Saturday night

I ce cream sundaes, getting up for school on Mondays

E arrings, trying on make-up, making each other smile

N ot today my parents say, see you maybe next Sunday

D ancing, drawing, we never have time for snoring

S weets in our pockets, sand in our shoes, holiday memories, so many to choose!

Anabel Maddison (10)

Nursery Hill Primary School, Nuneaton

Animals' Homes

From the highest peaks to the smallest dens,
All these animals have homes,
To the freezing Antarctic to the blistering desert
You can count loads.
Without these habitats where will we live?
Left there in the cold,
We will be left on our own to grow old,
Not with TVs or phones,
Just on our own.
No way to communicate through texts,
Just on our own.
Stop deforestation
So we're not alone anymore.

Will Smith (11)
Nursery Hill Primary School, Nuneaton

My Beloved Grandma

G randma, you were my bestest friend
R eally thought you'd be there till the end
A lways smiling and lots of fun
N ever cooked dinner as badly as my mum
D ancing to your favourite song
M any to choose from and some were long
A lways love you and that's no lie, I will always look for you in the sky.

Amy Kirby (11)
Nursery Hill Primary School, Nuneaton

Friends

F riends are helpful, caring and kind

R espect you

I always try to be there when they need me

E ncourage you

N o one can break our special bond

D eserve you

S pecial friends are hard to find, but when you do they are special forever.

Brooke Jones (10)
Nursery Hill Primary School, Nuneaton

Friends

F riends
R ight there when you need them
I n the darkest of days they are there with you
E ncourage you
N ever let you down
D eserve you
S omebody who cares about you.

Tiana Buckler (10)

Nursery Hill Primary School, Nuneaton

I Once Had A Strange Dream

I once had a strange dream
Where the grass was blue and the sky was green.
There were trees full of mountain goats
And they all wore strange coats.
My bed was covered in cream
And spiders and flies were on a team.

Jack Taylor (11)
Nursery Hill Primary School, Nuneaton

To The Zoo

To the zoo we go
With Mammi, Pappi and Lou.
We walk, we talk, we gawp,
There are lions and tigers, they stalk.

The bear with a length of hair,
Who wasn't there,
Appeared with quite a scare.

Isabelle Mellalieu (11)
Nursery Hill Primary School, Nuneaton

My Space Dream!

We live in a tiny fraction of it, there is so much more,
Beyond the lustrous stars, there's a universe to explore!
The burnished stars hide the skies,
Where your favourite rocket flies.

I dream of soaring out to space,
Proudly representing the human race.
I'd try and catch a star or two
And take in the indescribable view!

Earth is a special planet to share,
As well as the moon, we must take care.
Mars is our sister, used to be like us,
Luckily, the out-of-this-world asteroids haven't caused a ruckus.

Rebecca Evans (11)
Pentrepoeth Primary School, Bassaleg

The Phantom Murderer

"Help!" called the traveller,
After catching the phantom's gaze,
The withered phantom stood eerily,
The traveller's heart stuck in an endless maze.

The slender trees stood intimidatingly,
Offering no help this time,
The phantom started to close in,
For the listeners, there was no crime.

He hallucinated a loud bang,
Thinking it was help from a friend,
But his soul knew it was not saved from doom,
For this terror had no end.

The white glistening moon
Peered gently from the sky,
Listening very peacefully,
At the traveller's lonely cry.

Spooked, the petrified horse,
Thundered off through the trees,

Snorting very loudly,
Leaving his master to be ceased.

Exhausted, cold and scared,
The traveller saw an escape,
It was going to take some adrenaline,
But the traveller put his plan into shape.

He saw a door in a nearby cottage,
It would be the scariest but only way out,
The phantom took another step closer,
The traveller's reaction was only a shout.

Clueless, confused, petrified,
The traveller began to cry,
The phantom suddenly struck
And the silence returned to the night sky.

William Prendergast (11)
Pentrepoeth Primary School, Bassaleg

Gymnastics!

If you ping off the bar,
You can fly far.
I love the beam
And working as a team.
I may fly into the door
When I tumble on the floor.
You can do the vault
But don't get a fault.
I go flying high,
Jumping to the sky.
When I twist and turn
New moves I learn.
I love fantastic gymnastics!

Jemima Taylor (10)
Pentrepoeth Primary School, Bassaleg

Venus

Venus is the brightest object in the sky
At 250km high.

Venus is named after the Roman goddess of love
and beauty,
It's the brightest planet you can ever see.

Venus is sometimes called the Earth's sister,
But not a mister.

Venus is second from the sun
Like a honey bun.

Apple Davies (10)
Pentrepoeth Primary School, Bassaleg

Uranus

Uranus here,
I'm seventh from the sun,
I like to spend my days upside down, it's fun.
I'm nice and blue,
Maybe a tint of green,
But only my name sounds so supreme.
My home is quite different,
As you can see,
Some people mistake it,
If you know what I mean.

Eva Gulotta (10)
Pentrepoeth Primary School, Bassaleg

The Cat And The Mouse

There was a cat with a white patched eye,
Who pounced on his owner with a mouse nearby.
The mouse shuffled, muffled and scuffled about,
While the cat got stuck in the mouse's trap.
A piece of cheese dropped, which the mouse
quickly ate!
While the cat meowed, "Uh! Thank you mate!"
With a sigh in his eye, he said,
"I'll get you back, back in your trap!"
He wiggled free with a cat's flea,
The mouse was terrified with wide eyes
And said, "A meat-eater. A sleek sneaker. A
howling smile.
A cat running a million miles.
A cat's purr. A cat's pretty fur.
A hissing creature.
A silent feature.
Better run. Argh!"

Daisy Yardanova (8)
Seaton House School, Sutton

Space

A big, black, vast area dotted with stars,
With lots of planets in there including Mars.
The stars are winking and twinkling,
But nothing can be better than the sun.
It's bigger than Neptune, Earth and the moon,
Even Saturn can't get the fun!

Boiling, bubbling, burning anything in its path
With everything moving around it,
As if it's the king of the future and past.
It will never get overtaken because it's the
strongest of them all,
Nothing is hotter or fiercer, it also probably makes
sure!

Night-time, it's darker than ever,
Being lit up feebly by the moon and stars.
Daytime, you can't see the little glowers,
As though the sun has turned on
And the moon has turned off.

It's a mystery of what's waiting to be found in the unknown,
Who knows what lies in the depths of the solar system and Milky Ways.
Could it be aliens that are green with three eyes?
Or slime oozers that squirt out slime?
Or maybe, a new world with more and more life to be found?

Saamiya Choudhry (8)
Seaton House School, Sutton

My Gang, My Rules

Welcome to the gang
I'm so glad you're joining
Though if you don't like it
There is no withdrawing

You can be anything you dream of
As long as I decide
You can think of anything you want to
If your view's the same as mine
You can do anything you wish to do
But only if I say
You can do it whenever you please
As long as it's today
You can have as many as you fancy
As long as it's only one
You can laugh all you like
As long as you don't have fun
You can have whatever you desire
As long as it's under a pound
You can talk as much as you like
As long as you don't make a sound
You can travel around the world

As long as you don't go far
You can do everything that's possible
On second thoughts you can't

Now those are my simple rules
And I'm sure you will agree
That this gang is my gang
And this gang belongs to me.

Amelia Sims (11)

Seaton House School, Sutton

The Beach

The golden sand tickling your toes,
The little rock pools full of jellyfish glow,
The gentle waves going *lap, a lap, lap,*
The children building sandcastles, *tap, a tap, tap,*
People crazy, about to buy spades,
The grown-ups lazing about under sunshades.

The sand so smooth to dig in,
The sea so gorgeously blue.
The beach huts so vibrant and cute,
The sea and beach so vast and mute.
The fish so quick and fast, jumping high and low
The seaweed waving around tickling everyone's
toes.

The sun blazing down, burning the sand,
The sea too deep to see the bottom of land.
As night arrives people start leaving,
Laughter dies down, chatter comes to an end.
The sunset a comfortable orangey colour,
The sky turns to a purply-blue, star-filled river,
And the sand becomes cool.

Everybody loves the beach, which has two sides,
Both beautiful in every way.

Nabila Choudhry (8)
Seaton House School, Sutton

Flavoured Food At Lunchtime

Ring the chime! It's lunchtime!
I wonder what all the children are eating today,
Let's watch them all munch and chew away!

The sweet little girl is nibbling fairy cakes
And as sugary as sugar canes, treats and bakes.

The sour little boy is sucking a tangy lime,
Along with icy lemonade - he drinks it all the time!

The nerdy kids with glasses, don't dare to chew
molasses!
No crunch, crunch!
They munch carrots for the eyesight
And spinach for the might!

Then what about the bad-tempered girls?
Well they eat spicy curly whirls
And the famous Indian dish, Nihari.

With a side of sweet chilli roll
That's why they always have cloudy smoke
Coming out of their earhole!

Stomp, stomp, click, click, scurry, scurry,
Here comes the teacher of history
And she is eating the Roman -
Remember to do your homework curry!

Sahar Gulamali (10)

Seaton House School, Sutton

Bully

Call me a bully,
Call me as bad as sin,
But inside I'm all tangled up
And I can't let anyone in.

Call me horrid,
Avoid me like hell,
But this is my way
Of coping from inside.

I'm not proud of where I come from,
But it is all I've got
And I can't tell anyone
That I feel like rot.

And I can't tell anyone
Cos they'll cart me off,
But they can't, won't,
Cos my mum is all I've got.

I'm scared, frightened,
But I can't stop now,

No friends, no home,
What if I got into a row?

But I am only building a shell
Just to protect myself
From reality.

So if you hate me,
Avoid me,
See if I care.

Call me a bully,
Call me as bad as sin,
But inside I'm all tangled up
And I can't let anyone in.

Maeve Russell (10)
Seaton House School, Sutton

School

"Did you have a nice day at school, Amy?"
"Nothing special you know, but it really was crazy.

The dentist came and pulled out my tooth,
But really, it wasn't super loose.

I met a magician who sawed me in two
And I had to be stuck back together with glue.

On the way there, my umbrella broke
And I forgot to wear my raincoat.

I met a clown who wasn't funny,
Then he told me his name was actually Dunny.

Under my desk, there was a lot of gum
And I accidentally touched it with my thumb.

The food at school was very disgusting
So I don't think anyone was munching.

I was beaten at chess by the invisible mayor
When I looked in the mirror but I wasn't there.

That's it!"

"That's very nice dear, your dinner is ready."

Elyanna Oyediran (9)
Seaton House School, Sutton

Aliens At The Fairground

A colossal spaceship landed on the ground,
We were at the fairground,
A large crowd gathered round,
As my heart began to pound.

But not a sound,
Yet again?
I calmed down
And looked around,
We were safe and sound.

Lightly, something stepped on the ground,
Right behind the merry-go-round.
I felt like I was bound by my invisible ropes
And leisurely walked to the mound.

Where a jelly-like creature lay,
Its arms settled far away,
With multicoloured blisters plastered on its face,
There it will stay.

For eternity,
Till today.

Zahra Choudry (9)
Seaton House School, Sutton

My Clever Cat

My clever cat is as black as a chalkboard.
My clever cat is as quick as a flashing sword.
My clever cat loves to eat meat.
My clever cat always says bon appétit.
My clever cat can turn off the lights.
My clever cat always gives me a bite.
My clever cat always tries to scare me.
My clever cat is barely hairy.
My clever cat always steals my toy so I have to say,
"Oi, naughty boy."

Mila Lieu (7)
Seaton House School, Sutton

Late

8:31... We've just begun.
8:32... My sister's lost her shoe.
8:33... My mum's spilt her tea.
8:34... We need to get out the door.

8:35... I can't believe we're still alive.
8:36... My sister's picking up sticks.
8:37... We need a miracle from Heaven.
8:38... We're gonna be late.
8:39... We've got one minute in time.

8:40... We're late.

Hannah Hassan (10)
Seaton House School, Sutton

The Rainbow

Red like an apple, crispy and crunchy.
Orange as a sunset, when the day ends.
Yellow like the sparkling sunshine, gleaming
brightly on your neck.
Green as the summer's grass which tickles my toes.
Blue like the sea of sky, high above my head.
Indigo like blueberries, juicy and sweet.
Violet like fields of sweet-smelling lavender.
Many colours.
One rainbow.

Ella Erasmus (8)
Seaton House School, Sutton

Quicksand

I woke up in quicksand under my bed,
The more I struggle on my bed
The more I sink.

The more I relax
The more I float.

The more I try
The more I sink.

The more I stay still
The more I float.

The more I pull
The more I sink.

Suddenly I escaped
And realised it was a dream.

Elise Moore-Arthur (9)
Seaton House School, Sutton

Me

Hello, it's me, Sophia,
I am eight years old
And I am hard-working.
I have lots of colours that are my favourite such
as...
Blue, red, brown and so on...
I am very lucky to have such wonderful friends,
Parents and relatives.
I like art and I smile
Like the shining, bright, wonderful sun.

Sophia Saeed (8)
Seaton House School, Sutton

My Adventures About Animals!

A n elegant swan swimming gracefully,

N aughty monkeys playing cheeky tricks,

I gloos and penguins are so cute, especially baby ones,

M ammoths and elephants are similar but live in different places,

A peacock as colourful as a rainbow,

L eopards are fast, as fast as a person

A ntelopes eat ants and different insects,

D inosaurs are real but they are extinct.

V icious tigers and lions are scary.

E ven giraffes are enormous and tall.

N ature and animals are amazing and cool.

T he different types of animals are scary, quiet or fast.

U nbearably cute animals, so fluffy.

R ainbow parrots and different birds,

E ven animals can be scared just like us!

Makeda Williamson (8)

St Andrew's CE Primary School, Plymouth

Animal Types

A ll animals have a group, some are soft, some are rough!

N o animal is the same, some of them are really tough!

I nsects come in all shapes and sizes but lots are very small,

M ammals are born not out of eggs,

A ll fish can swim but they don't have long legs!

L ions have long manes like flowing fiery rivers!

T abby cats are stripy and soft,

Y ou might find a bat hiding in the loft!

P lease look after all animals big and small,

E agles are huge flying birds,

S cary buffalos come in big herds.

Hannah Ryder (8)
St Andrew's CE Primary School, Plymouth

The Seasons

T he winter is frosty and cold, the holly's freezing up,

H ot summer ice creams melting, butterflies fluttering,

E very autumn leaf falls lightly in the wind.

S pring so pretty as the blossoms grow so pink like bows,

E very winter is fun, Christmas comes, so fun!

A fter summer winter comes so cold but fun.

S o fun, so cool, so festival fun,

O h so fun, they start all over again.

N ever ends, always starts again,

S easons, seasons, so fun to have.

Rihanna Voronina (8)
St Andrew's CE Primary School, Plymouth

All The Animals

My favourite animal...
Cheetahs zooming around the grass and licking their fur.

When I go to the zoo I can see...
A buffalo stampeding around behind the glass.

When I got to the zoo I can see...
A gorilla trying to smash the glass. *Bang!*

When I got to the zoo I can see...
Giraffes eating the leaves from the trees.

When I got to the zoo I can see...
Zebras zooming along the grass.

When I got to the zoo I can see...
Owls flying in the bright blue sky.

Zylah Ford (8)
St Andrew's CE Primary School, Plymouth

About My Family

M y family are the closest people to me,
Y et they're very, very kind to me.

F riends of mine are always in my family,
A ll my family are important to me,
M y family are like machines working for me all
the time,
I can always rely on my family,
L oving and kind in anything I do,
Y ou're the best family ever!

Loveday Hoskin (7)
St Andrew's CE Primary School, Plymouth

Alien!

Because of what the astronomers could see
They felt as though they were about to flee
They could see a white star coming at us
It was about to be the size of a bus
They could see a green figure at the top
They thought as though their eyes were about to pop
Then something came down, it was wearing a crown...
An *alien!*
Everyone was saying their prayers
As they were running to their lairs
As everybody did what the alien pleased
Some drunken man said, "Throw the cheese!"
So everybody did so and the alien said, "No!"
And so the alien went back home
In his fancy little dome
Everybody cheered as they peered
At the alien!

Eric Paqvalen (10)
St Mary's CE Junior School, Twickenham

Rivers And Oceans

The magical liquid that is essential to all life on
Earth
Water has created our world and all birth

Oceans, rivers and lakes
Now there are much higher stakes
Since humans are taking over
Like their big, polluting Land Rovers
Now is the time to act
Make haste and look at the facts!

The Pacific, the Atlantic and the Arctic too
Are being polluted by humans, what can we do?
The oceans are filled with animals galore
More than you'd ever find at a food store
See the tropical coral reef
And you'll be saddened with disbelief
There are plastic bags in every one
It really is no fun

Microfibres, chemicals and Styrofoam
Are destroying their underwater homes

Persistent plastic bottles and cups
Are hurting adorable seal pups
Turtles are being injured by straws
Oil spills up to the polar bears' paws
Whales are tricked into eating plastic bags
Why are we acting like scallywags?

Reduce, reuse, recycle and refuse
Only buy the things that you can actually use
Choose organic and sustainable fish
Think about everything that goes into your dish
Walk, don't drive or fly
These are the beliefs to live your life by

Preserve, conserve and save
Don't become a consumerist slave!

Amaya Maqsood (9)
St Mary's CE Junior School, Twickenham

If I Could Do Anything...

If I could do anything...
I would leap over bridges
And run about all day.
I'd help my friends and family.
When they come to stay.

I would read my teacher's mind
And tell them what to do.
I'd take over the whole school
And make ghosts that go, "Boo!"

If I could do anything...
I would ban grown-ups
And fly to the moon.
I'd talk to all the planets
And play them my new tune.

I would lift up buildings
And soar through the air.
I'd climb up walls
And build a secret lair.

If I could do anything...
I would ride on shooting stars
And play games with the weather.
I'd be rich as rich
And able to afford leather.

I would live with my friends
And tell them my powers.
I'd have a big library
And three huge towers.

If I could do anything...
I would know everything
And pass every test.
My teachers would praise me
And say I should know less.

But if I couldn't do anything,
I'd still be happy with my life,
Just as long as I didn't get hurt by a knife.

Luciana Nico Siddique Bottomly (10)
St Mary's CE Junior School, Twickenham

The Unicorn That Wasn't There

A girl lay in bed, eyes tight shut
Dreaming of a book she had read that day
She felt a tickle on the back of her neck
And heard a strange snort at the end of her bed

She opened her eyes but it was hard to see
Was that a shadow on her bedroom wall?
The girl slowly rolled to the side of her bunk
And found herself facing a perfectly white face

The face had a horn on the top of its head
With a spiral rising up it, in a rainbow colour
As she slowly sat up and looked to the floor
She saw four cloven hooves on long, white legs

At the end of a body was a fluffy rainbow tail
The colours were magnificent and lit up the walls
A mane ran down to the nape of her neck
Flowing like a river of sparkling pink

From that day on, she received visits each week
Until her tenth birthday when the unicorn just
disappeared
It stopped coming, stopped being there at all
After a while, she stopped believing in the unicorn

She believed it was never real and that it was a
dream
But far away, the unicorn knew that indeed, she
was real.

Euan Offord (9)
St Mary's CE Junior School, Twickenham

This Strange Planet

Boom! My rocket hits the ground
I clamber out and examine this new planet
Everyone has just two arms and legs
And no antennae at all!

It's so strange there,
They eat funny food
Like those long, tomatoey strings
They call it spaghetti and slurp it up
But I can't, it's so difficult to eat!

They put on funny things called clothes
Which vary from T-shirts to leggings
But I have one word to describe all of them...
Itchy!

They drive in weird pods called 'cars'
And cars don't even hover!
They just slide along the ground on things called 'wheels'
What a curious way to travel!

Well, If I'm going to be stuck on this planet,
I'd better get used to their ways
But I can't seem to get anything they do *right*
I can't count, can't read, can't write
I crashed the car thirty times
(I think, did I mention I can't count?)
And science... I just don't understand!

I really want to go home.

Anna Wilkinson (9)
St Mary's CE Junior School, Twickenham

Planet Rhyming Call

Eight planets around the sun
Listen as I call each one
Mercury here, number one,
Which is the closest planet to the sun
Venus here, number two
Just shining bright like it's new!
Earth here, number three
Earth is home to you and me!
Mars here, number four
Hottest planet of them all
Jupiter here, number five,
Let me guess who's next in line
Saturn here, number six
With rings of dust and cold ice that mix
Uranus here, number seven
A planet just high up in Heaven
Neptune here, number eight
Now I'm done, wait... wait
Am I forgetting one?
Yes, there's Pluto too
The dwarf one

Very small, very smooth
Just like a boom and a poem one too
Bye-bye now, it's the end
I know you've had fun reading my poem,
Now I'm done, hope you had fun!

Gloria Makufi (10)
St Mary's CE Junior School, Twickenham

The Space Vortex

The infinite darkness of space
Is a truly horrible place
So it's no wonder that
The human race does not explore it

"Why?"

Because under those planets and stars
Which people can't catch in large jars
Lies an endless vacuum
You cannot kick or lift or pour it

"Why not?"

As it's just a ginormous mass
Of gas, some atoms and more gas
You can't move it around
This strange substance is called dark matter

"What else?"

People have gone to the moon
They took off an hour before noon

But they paid no attention
All they did was stand and natter

"Oh!"

In a word, space is a vortex.

Alexander F E Harrison (9)
St Mary's CE Junior School, Twickenham

My Neighbour And Her Dogs

My neighbour has a lot of dogs
They like to fetch massive logs
The fluffy poodles love their noodles
The bouncy pugs love their hugs
All the dogs are up for larks
With wagging tails and lots of barks.

Willow is a feisty beagle
He spends his day chasing seagulls!
Cassy is a Great Dane
She loves a walk down the lane
All the dogs are energetic
Some unfit, some athletic!

Billy is a Jack Russell
Who loves to have a little tussle
Fluffy the pomeranian is always happy
She jumps around being yappy
All the dogs love a puddle
But I prefer a warm snuggle.

Sienna Mary Dane (9)
St Mary's CE Junior School, Twickenham

The Wonderful Lives Of Animals

The lives of animals are not what you think
Do they sleep all day?
Do they only stick around with us as we give them food?
The answer is no
They cuddle us when we're sad
And play with us when we're happy
But when the clock strikes twelve
Things are different
As cute as a newborn baby
They trot off to a secret garden
In the heart of the forest
Animals live the lives that humans do
Dogs dive
Cats cook
Rabbits row
Horses hedgefund
But is all this true?
Is it really what happens?
There's only one way to find out.

Rosie Mcmullen (10)
St Mary's CE Junior School, Twickenham

Into The Night

When I look up into the night,
I believe I can take flight,
Into Zeus' domain!

When I look down on the Earth,
I wonder how Gaia gave birth,
To titans twelve that trust in pain...

The stars in their constellations wink at me,
I want to understand how they came to be
And all of their names...

As I zoom past Pegasus and Cassiopeia,
Their beauty draws me very near
Am I on a starlit train?

Now Hemera brings the start of a new day
Her lights illuminate my way,
How I can't wait for the night again!

Charlotte Irvine (9)
St Mary's CE Junior School, Twickenham

Into Space

As I get into the rocket,
I feel the excitement rush through my body
I see the crowds of people cheering me on
I smell the food being made for the event
I hear the engines of the rocket ready to blast off
I taste the sweet tang of my last meal on my
tongue

As I blast off,
I feel the pressure of the speed
I see my colleagues working on the controls
I smell the sweet smell of oxygen in my lungs
I hear the deep rumble coming from the engines
I taste the remains of my sandwich in my mouth

I am finally in space!

Marco Gonzalez (9)
St Mary's CE Junior School, Twickenham

Locus (Space In Latin)

There are nine planets
That orbit the sun
But people and animals
Just live on one.

The Earth is our planet
We must take good care
Of the air, land and water
That people must share.

A rocket is the best way
To travel in space
With one great big blast
You can go any place.

The sun keeps us warm
Wherever we are
All our light comes
From this great big star.

Astronauts travel
A long way through space

They learn lots of facts
That they bring back to base.

Lucy Goddin (10)
St Mary's CE Junior School, Twickenham

What Will Space Be Like In The Future?

In the future, the solar system will change
Mars will turn around Earth
And Jupiter will turn around Mars
Saturn will turn around Jupiter and so on...

But most important is Mars!
Mars will turn around Earth 1,000,000 times faster
Than the moon turns around Earth
Can you believe it?

People will be able to go to Neptune as fast as light
And Mars will be called the big bright star,
Very hot and big
People will be able to breathe in space
Without air or oxygen!
How amazing will that be?

Ibuki Miyaji (9)
St Mary's CE Junior School, Twickenham

My Out Of This World Fear

I have a fear
It's about something not near here
I fear little green men plotting to come near
Then they zoom, not furious but friendly
Maybe my fear is not real
Maybe I could make friends with these creatures
Day after day, I make one more green friend
After that, we show them our ways
They act like dogs and we play all day
That's why you don't always have to trust fear
Maybe it's all just up there, you never know.

Gabriel Le Boiteux (9)
St Mary's CE Junior School, Twickenham

Save The World

Here's a message you all should know
The environment is your friend, not your foe
Loggers are destroying and cutting the growth
Recycle, reuse, you need to do both
Our air is polluted, we need to do something
But right now, all we're doing is nothing
Plastic ends up in our oceans
For turtles, it's nothing but a deadly potion
Minibeasts and creatures are ending their lives
I don't think we'll make it to 2045.

Alba Morrison (10)
St Mary's CE Junior School, Twickenham

The Journey

I'm going on a trip,
I bite my bottom lip,
I'm rocketing to space,
To save the human race.

I see stars,
I see Mars,
I see the names of chocolate bars,
Galaxy, Milky Way,
I even had one yesterday.

The rings of Saturn,
The stars make a pattern,
The heat of the sun,
The comets run.

I feel small,
But I stand up tall,
I'm on a quest,
I must not rest.

Bibi Foxwood (9)
St Mary's CE Junior School, Twickenham

Is Anybody Out There?

Billions of millions of stars
Not just the sun
Is anybody out there?
There should be lots
Are they like us?
Or are they green?
Do they drink tea?
Do they even drink anything?
We would love to meet them
I wonder what they're like
Maybe they like to invade
Maybe they live in countries
Just how would we come to meet?
Give them a call?
Now I'm not sure about inviting them to Earth.

Max Tanawin Attwood (9)
St Mary's CE Junior School, Twickenham

Spaceships

S paceships flying through the sky

P ieces of asteroids up, up high

A liens who live on Mars

C ould just reach the stars

E clipse every four years

S tars can also appear

H ot, hot sun

I wish I could fly so high, it would be so much fun

P luto may not be a planet but Mercury is a planet

S adly, I am not an astronaut, but I've learnt a lot!

Daniel Hammer (10)
St Mary's CE Junior School, Twickenham

What Am I?

I can be big
I can be small
I can be a magician
Or do I exist at all?

Can I walk?
Can I talk?
Can I even eat from a fork
Or can I do the moonwalk?

Can I fit into your shoe?
Can my body turn blue?
Do you think I'll eat you
Or maybe turn into you?

I guess it's time to reveal myself, but first one more clue
I am a shape-shifter too, I am an alien shape-shifter.

Mollie-Rae Mo (9)
St Mary's CE Junior School, Twickenham

Where Could This Creature Be From?

One day, I was in my room
It was a full moon

Stars up so bright
Although darker than night

I heard a strange noise
It was a creature doing a pose

It looked fluffy and bright
This situation was tight

This creature wasn't that spooky
So I named her Suzy

This creature said a weird word
But I knew that this creature was out of this world.

Lal Kuruyazici (10)
St Mary's CE Junior School, Twickenham

Jupiter

J ust as it appears, it's the biggest planet of all

U nexpectedly, it comes with a brown and grey colour

P eering through the galaxy, it shines like a star

I t is the most adored planet

T o other people, it is tiny but to us, it's huge

E nter onto the planet, if you dare, be amazed

R ough and bold, it stands out bright.

Owen Minty (9)

St Mary's CE Junior School, Twickenham

The Depths Of Darkness

The silence in the endless void ripples through the
inky dark
Celestial fire that burns from above, spitting
uncontrollably blinding sparks
In the far north, a swirling spiral of light came from
above
Guiding through with the lights that we all love
Our giant, burning guardians that show us through
the night
The precious intergalactic direct us with stars that
shine bright.

Izzy Mortimore (10)

St Mary's CE Junior School, Twickenham

The Blazing Bush

The thing that's bad is the blazing bush
The blazing bush does nothing but push
The blazing bush is a horrible thing
The fire engines are going, *bing bong bing!*
People choke when they breathe the smoke
Marsupials fry when they can't see the sky
If we don't act now our Earth will die
Help us save our planet
From the blazing bush fire.

Elise Cobb (10)

St Mary's CE Junior School, Twickenham

London

London pays with single pounds
Little pennies can be found
London, in the corner of the UK
There will be bank holidays in May
Big Ben makes me feel so small
London makes me feel so high
Royal Albert makes me feel so excited
Buckingham Palace makes me feel so royal
The Union Jack makes me feel so proud
London makes me feel like my favourite place to go.

Frankie Montero (9)
St Mary's CE Junior School, Twickenham

Where Is My...?

Where is my bike?
Is it in the shed?
Is it under the bed?
Is it in a pit?
Oh! It's where I left it

Where is my dog?
Is he in my pocket?
Perhaps in an electrical socket?
Is he in the shed?
Oh! He's on his bed

Where is my pen?
Is it under a hen?
That would give me a laugh
Oh! It's on my head.

Federico Prenovost (10)
St Mary's CE Junior School, Twickenham

Space Playground

Can you do the moonwalk,
Then dance across the stars?
Will you slide along the Milky Way,
Then somersault around Mars?
Hide-and-seek among the planets
Spin around Saturn's ring
Juggle with Jupiter and Neptune
Then over to Venus, you can swing
Catch an eclipse of the sun
Then ride a satellite home.

Martha Swift (9)
St Mary's CE Junior School, Twickenham

Galaxy

Looking up at the sky at night
Staring at the beautiful sight
Walking with my family
Wondering about the galaxy.

Hoping to see the Milky Way
As soon as we see the moon, we lay,
Watching it we see the stars
And peeking out the planet Mars.

Oh, the beauty of the universe!

Peter Deasy (10)
St Mary's CE Junior School, Twickenham

Liverpool

Liverpool are my favourite team
They're very hard to beat
We won the World Club cup
And the same year, the Champions League
We beat Barca 4-0
And Anfield is a thrill
Anfield is their fortress
It's where they play best
It's where they're sure to put Man U to the test.

Ben John (10)
St Mary's CE Junior School, Twickenham

The Wonders Of Space

S pace is a wonderful place to be

P lanets are epic, an amazing sight to see

A steroids are large and rare to be found

C osmos you will find in the galaxy around

E arth is our planet, so please keep it clean. We don't want to die and no longer be seen!

Josh Menassa Tye (10)

St Mary's CE Junior School, Twickenham

Space?

S ince I was in space there was no gravity.
P ulling the emergency break lever was terrifying.
A t last, I completed the mission Mars 37.
C alling the space station was so exciting.
E ventually, I woke up, was it a dream?

Matvey Yasser (10)
St Mary's CE Junior School, Twickenham

Stars In Space

S tars are beautiful, stars are bright
P lenty of stars there are to look at night
A mazing planets, wonderful moon
C ame to space to have some fun
E nter and run all the way to the sun.

Camila Key Bianchin (9)

St Mary's CE Junior School, Twickenham

The Monster

Two heads, six eyes and has one big foot,
He roams in the shadows, he roams in the night,
He's vicious because he bites, his name is Yight,
He eats little kids, beware of Yight,
Beware, he's very real!

Poppy Frances Victoria Drew (9)

St Mary's CE Junior School, Twickenham

Venus

V ery hot.
E normously waiting to be discovered.
N ext to Mercury in the solar system.
U nanimously the bets planet by far.
S pacious and endlessly hot.

Heitor Rucco Turina (10)
St Mary's CE Junior School, Twickenham

Space

S is for shining stars
P is for planets like Pluto
A is for angry aliens
C is for colossal craters on the moon
E is for exciting space.

Tai-Rhys Anthony Brown (10)
St Mary's CE Junior School, Twickenham

Awesome Adventure!

I want to find a dragon, I want a tiger,
I'll fly on a great griffin higher and higher.
I will explore a volcano,
I will climb a rainbow.
Adventure here we come!

I'll find treasure,
The tallest building is what I will measure.
I'll go in a magical shed,
Then I will find a world under my bed.
Adventure here we come!

I'll find a cold black hole,
I will find a troll.
I'll see the world,
Then I'll warm the cold.
Adventure here we come!

I'm tired but I want to sleep,
Happily ever after we meet.
I'll tell my story to the whole world,
Adventure has come to an end!

Grace Dada (9)
St Thomas CE Primary School, Boston

Disneyland Is A Magical Place

Disneyland is a magical place,
Smiles can be seen on every face,
Characters, rides, shops and more,
An amazing time will be had for sure,
Something magical can be found,
By following Tink's pixie dust sound,
If you bump into a genie
Don't be afraid for he's no meanie,
Be sure to visit Princess Pavillion,
The experience is one in a million,
When we're on Big Thunder Mountain,
Smile for the camera after the fountain,
When we get off Dad says, "Nutella crêpe?"
Guaranteed we all say yep,
When we leave I shed a tear,
But I know we'll be back next year,
Disneyland is a magical place!

Isabelle Gutteridge (9)
St Thomas CE Primary School, Boston

The Dragon

Mortal, monstrous, the dragon mouth is,
Noxious, destructive and deadly,
Ravaging, ruinous, the dragon tail is,
Murderous, damaging and catastrophic.

Beady, mesmerising, the dragon is,
Fire-filled, fierce and infuriating,
Leathery, strapping, the dragon wing is,
Burly, brawning and terminal.

Life-threatening, fatal, the dragon breath is,
Inferno, conflagration and holocaust,
Keen, abominable, the dragon horn is,
Immense, savage and barbarous.

Muscly, durable, the dragon leg is,
Firm, powerful and robust,
Bloodthirsty, vicious the dragon is,
Homicidal, brutal and precious.

Lyla Needham (9)
St Thomas CE Primary School, Boston

The Tiger, Rabbit And Kitten Poem

Tiger
A tiger has magnificent bristly fur like a hairbrush.
Its got ink-black, wavy, thunder-black stripes.
A tiger's nose has straight down orange fur
And pink, bright like a pig's skin.

Kitten
A ginger kitten has misty white stripes.
The fur of a kitten is soft velvet.
Their ears are as straight as a spine.
A kitten's claws are as sharp as a sword.
Its nose is as pink as a flower.

Rabbit
A snowy rabbit is as white as the clouds.
The eyes are bright red and they look evil.
Their ears are straight like a knife.

Ella Farmer (10)
St Thomas CE Primary School, Boston

You

You are unique, important and special,
You are the best, never doubt yourself,
You are beautiful, just the way you are,
Magic, spectacular, beautiful, yes, that's who you are.

Imagine you are in Disneyland,
It's beautiful just like you,
Have as much fun as you like,
Just like we do when we see you.

Look in a mirror, what do you see?
Someone magical, well guess what? That is you.
Don't let people judge you,
You are you and nothing will change that.

Jessica Roofe (9)
St Thomas CE Primary School, Boston

Potion

As hot as burning fire,
A bursting purple potion,
Bubbling in a pot,
As purple as a raspberry,
Another as green as the ocean,
Bubbling, burning, squirting.

Spitting hot dots of green
In a pot that's very clean,
Foaming in the tub
And foaming in the air,
Crumbling, tumbling drips,
Bubbling, burning, squirting.

Slimy, gooey, gluey,
The water blue potion,
Full of glam from the ocean.

Lily Cowell (9)
St Thomas CE Primary School, Boston

Unique Creatures

Husky dogs are friendly,
They have a grey, white and puffy coat of fur.
Husky dogs are warm, soft and fluffy,
They have sky-blue eyes that spread like the deep ocean.

Rabbits are tiny,
They have a tail like a pom-pom.
Rabbits have thick fur,
They have long and soft ears.

Alsatians are cute,
They have pointy ears like a pencil.
Alsatians are adorable,
They have inky-black shadow eyes.

Libby-Jo Hurford (10)
St Thomas CE Primary School, Boston

Angels

The glowing magic halo is as bright as the sun,
It stays onto the soft ginger hair of an angel,
But the most unusual things about halos...
Are they like to have fun.

Fly, fly, the fluttering wings cry,
Soar the fresh, summer breeze.
But the question we all ask,
They are as light as a feather, why?

Oh, so sparkly and so bright,
It is the dress of her dreams,
Alright!

Lola Ward (9)
St Thomas CE Primary School, Boston

Huskies

Huskies, huskies don't be shy,
Fluffy fur, white as snow.
White underbelly like a beard,
Huskies everywhere!

Might think they're hypnotic
But bushy friends they are.
Endless pupils which stare mysteriously,
Huskies everywhere!

Huskies can bite,
White as knives.
Teeth like sharks,
Huskies everywhere!

Summer Parrott (9)
St Thomas CE Primary School, Boston

Plane

As a plane goes past,
Zoom, zoom, zoom,
It goes everywhere
Like a car.

It will deliver people,
Zoom, zoom, zoom,
At their destination,
Where they want.

As it lands,
Zoom, zoom, zoom,
It will go fast,
Then hold on tight.

Stephen Williams (9)
St Thomas CE Primary School, Boston

Our Journey Into Outer Space

When we travelled to outer space
We went and saw the moon!
Near Jupiter and Mars,
Near Saturn and Neptune
We saw an object from far away,
It looked like some sort of dish!
As smooth as glass!
As white as ivory!
It sat as a pearl on a trail of Saturn's rings!

As soon as I looked out of my window,
I saw a peering face,
It looked quite sly,
As sly as a snake,
Suddenly a light flashed,
The next second it was gone.
I didn't know what caused this,
But I just moved on into outer space...

Then I finally reached my destination,
The edge of space,
After all these years of wondering,
I still wonder who that is.

Natalia Ogorzalek (9)
Wharton Primary School, Little Hulton

The Boy At The Back Of The Line

There I stand, at the back of the line.
No friends, alone again, at the back of the line.
Dreaming of a friend, at the back of the line.
Along comes a boy, maybe he's the friend from my daydreams?
"Hi, I'm Brian, the boy at the back of the line."
There he stands at the back of the line.
No friends, alone again, at the back of the line.
"You don't have to be a boy at the back of the line."
Now it's time for us to shine at the back of the line.

Jamie-Luke Georgiou (10)
Wharton Primary School, Little Hulton

The Midnight Sky

Behold the midnight sky,
As beautiful as a firefly,
Rockets shooting through the clouds,
Oh that noise is so loud.

Behold the midnight sky,
Shooting stars shooting by,
Lunar is a glistening light
And it's always oh so bright.

Behold the midnight sky,
Flying by as quick as a star,
Auroras are so light,
As foggy as the moonlight.

Behold the midnight sky,
Stars shimmer as bright as a diamond.

Ethan Anderton (9)
Wharton Primary School, Little Hulton

The Shimmering Sky

Behold the shimmering sky,
As shiny as a firefly,
Shimmering, shining, shooting stars,
As they fluently glide past Mars.

Behold the shimmering sky,
Comets shooting through the night,
Oh my, what a beautiful sight.

Behold the shimmering sky,
Earth on Earth spins round,
Spinning till it hits the ground.

Behold the shimmering sky,
As beautiful as a butterfly.

Jesmira Kanjinga (10)
Wharton Primary School, Little Hulton

Twinkling Stars

Twinkling stars shining high
Like a diamond in the sky,
Floating all around,
Rockets shooting from the ground.

Twinkling stars shining high
While I sing you a lullaby,
Travelling along the Milky Way
Shouting, "I'm on my way!"

Twinkling stars shining high,
Earth is an apple in my eye.
Stars are shining oh so bright
In the middle of the night.

Amy Hricova (10)
Wharton Primary School, Little Hulton

Planets In The Sky

Planets roaming in the sky,
Like Neptune, oh so high.
All the time stars shine
Like diamonds hanging from a line.

Planets roaming in the sky,
Seeing a rocket flying by.
Shooting stars flying high,
Watching them makes me cry.

Planets roaming in the sky,
Sitting under the clouds is so high.
Aura lights are so bright,
Like flying a kite all night.

Harli Oxton (9)
Wharton Primary School, Little Hulton

The Gorgeous Galaxy

Rockets zooming in the sky,
It makes me want to cry.
Sun shining in the day,
Wonder what it is like in space.

Asteroids racing through the sky,
Up oh so high.
Comets crashing in the crater,
The moon will come out later.

Look up at night,
Aurora colours shining so bright.
So beautiful I could cry,
It is all in the sky.

Logan Pendlebury (10)
Wharton Primary School, Little Hulton

Space And Sky

Look in the sky,
Imagine being able to fly.
See all the planets and stars
And look at beautiful red Mars.

Look in the sky,
The Milky Way is so high.
Look in the air,
The Aurora and its dancing flare.

Look in the sky,
Shooting comets flying by.
Glistening stars up in space
Making it a magnificent place.

Thomas Kennedy (10)
Wharton Primary School, Little Hulton

The Sky

Look up at the sky,
Glorious stars oh so high.
Northern lights
Shining so bright.
Look up at the sky,
See a rocket flying by.
Our moon so big and round,
So far from the ground.
Look up at the sky,
So beautiful I could cry.
Gaze at the planet in space,
It is just an amazing place.

Jack Hamilton (10)
Wharton Primary School, Little Hulton

Swamp Seeker

Let me tell you about a mythical creature,
It kidnaps children and feeds on blood and bones.

It lives in water and lurks below the depths,
Stalking prey and kidnapping unsuspecting souls.

With its slimy scales, powerful arms and sharp claws,
It harvests disgusting gore.

Harlie Penny (10)
Wharton Primary School, Little Hulton

The Whale

Under the sea
Where nobody goes,
Lives a creature that everyone knows.
Deep within the ocean
Singing its songs,
Lives a whale where it truly belongs.
Swimming with its friends
And having fun,
Charting the oceans
As it always has been done!

Sheba Adebambo (10)
Wharton Primary School, Little Hulton

My Favourite Book Is...

A kennings poem

My favourite book is...

A page-flicker,
A word-holder,
An information-sharer,
A storyteller,
An imagination-giver,
An intelligence-lover,
A liquid-hater,
A bookshelf-survivor.

Yes, that's my favourite book!

Shema Ngarambe (10)

Wharton Primary School, Little Hulton

Cool Comets

C omes without a warning

O ut of nowhere

M eteors are even amazed

E xtraordinary sight to see

T he path is shaking when it lands

S ome people will call it an amazing sight to see like the red planet, Mars.

Sophia Cahill (9)
Wharton Primary School, Little Hulton

Brownie The Dog

A kennings poem

A tail-chaser,
A cat-hater,
A twig-lover,
A loud-barker,
A chicken-chomper,
A great growler,
A ball-catcher,
A finger-nibbler,
A fast runner.

Seanna Heidi Puddoo (9)

Wharton Primary School, Little Hulton

A Monster

A kennings poem

A fish-eater,
A shark-attacker,
A sunlight-hater,
A night-hunter,
A long sleeper,
A nightmare-creature,
A water-lover,
A children-chomper.

Julia Vernan (9)
Wharton Primary School, Little Hulton

Strange Creatures

High up in the sky,
Lives strange creatures that can fly.
They are not from this world,
But from outer space
And they live
In a magical place!

Elle-May Riley (9)

Wharton Primary School, Little Hulton

The Shark!

A kennings poem

A fish-eater,
A water-liver,
A fin-outer,
A human-stalker,
A night-roamer,
A day-roamer,
A water-swimmer,
A deep diver.

Callum D'arcy (9)
Wharton Primary School, Little Hulton

The Loch Ness Monster

A kennings poem

A mythical creature,
A lake-lover,
A fish-eater,
A fast swimmer,
A lonely creature,
A historic monster,
A Scottish myth.

Lucian Winder (9)
Wharton Primary School, Little Hulton

The Super Snake

A kennings poem

A sly slitherer,
A camouflaging superstar,
A climbing tube,
A meat-eater,
A skin-shedder,
A cage-hater,
A super spy.

William Szelepa (10)

Wharton Primary School, Little Hulton

YOUNG WRITERS INFORMATION

We hope you have enjoyed reading this book – and that you will continue to in the coming years.

If you're a young writer who enjoys reading and creative writing, or the parent of an enthusiastic poet or story writer, do visit our website **www.youngwriters.co.uk**. Here you will find free competitions, workshops and games, as well as recommended reads, a poetry glossary and our blog. There's lots to keep budding writers motivated to write!

If you would like to order further copies of this book, or any of our other titles, then please give us a call or order via your online account.

Young Writers
Remus House
Coltsfoot Drive
Peterborough
PE2 9BF
(01733) 890066
info@youngwriters.co.uk

Join in the conversation!
Tips, news, giveaways and much more!

 YoungWritersUK   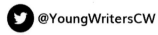 @YoungWritersCW